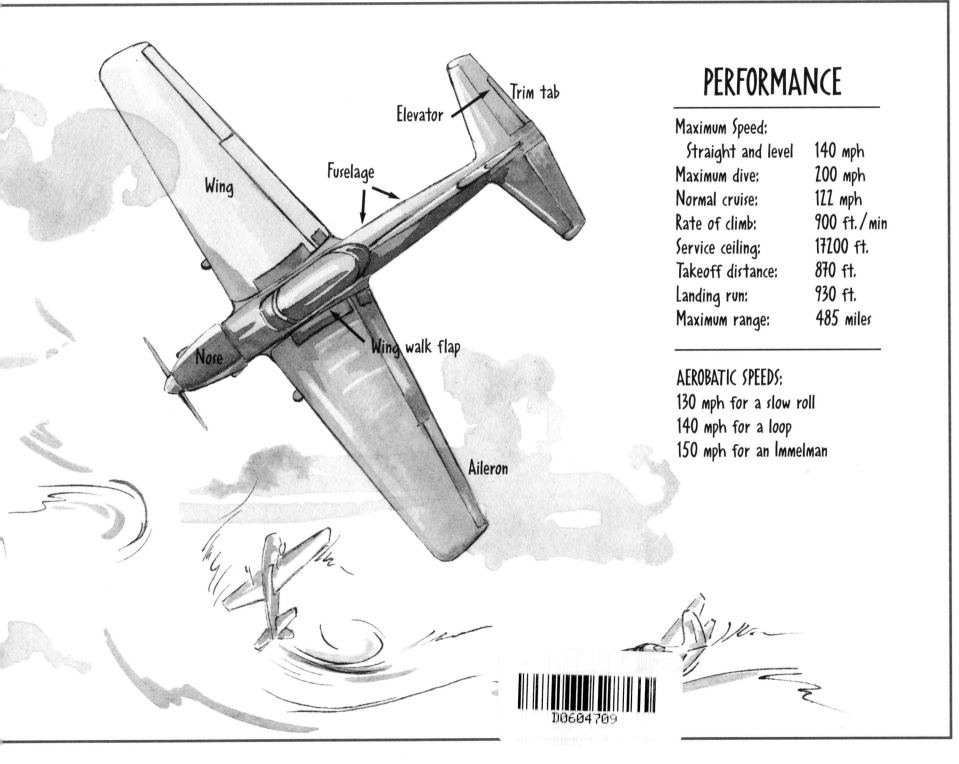

Trim tab

Elevator

Fuselage

Wing

Nose

Wing walk flap

Aileron

PERFORMANCE

Maximum Speed:
Straight and level   140 mph
Maximum dive: 200 mph
Normal cruise: 122 mph
Rate of climb: 900 ft./min
Service ceiling: 17200 ft.
Takeoff distance: 870 ft.
Landing run: 930 ft.
Maximum range: 485 miles

AEROBATIC SPEEDS:

130 mph for a slow roll
140 mph for a loop
150 mph for an Immelman

C-GR⊕WL

The Daring Little Airplane

July 24, 2004

NAT McHAFFIE

To Rachel,

Blue Skies

Nat

Vanwell Publishing Limited

St. Catharines, Ontario

Beautiful.
Sharp black nose pointing at the sky.
Long tapered wings, bright yellow, shining in the sun.

That sharp rounded tail looks like all the de Havilland relatives in England.
The English cousins were named for moths: Gypsy Moth, Fox Moth, Tiger Moth.
The Canadians will be native animals.
Otter? Beaver? Not quite. Buffalo? Definitely not!
Ah – of course! C-Growl is small and nimble.

Ladies and Gentlemen, the Chipmunk!

De Havilland Canada Number One is ready for its first flight.
It's a clear summer morning on the wide windy airport hill and everyone is looking.

> Pat, the test pilot, does C-GROWL's preflight checklist for the first time.
> > Switch the Ground to FLIGHT – that connects the batteries.
> > Turn the Fuel to ON – that opens the line from the tank.
> > Push the Primer, one, two, three – that pumps a little fuel into the engine.
> > Open the Throttle – half an inch is plenty.
> Pat shouts "CLEAR!" and everyone steps back from the propeller.
> He pulls the starter ring and Whu-Whu-WhuHHrrr – the engine comes alive with a loud growl.
>
> | | |
> |---|---|
> | Oil pressure? | Check. |
> | Engine electricity? | Check. |
> | Ailerons and elevators responding? | Check. |

C-GROWL taxis out, waggling from side to side so the pilot can see around the nose.

At the runway there's a pause as if the plane is taking a big breath. Smoothly Pat adds power, lifts the tail, speeds faster and faster down the runway until magically, gently, the Chipmunk is flying.

Pat starts carefully with only a little roll, a little yaw and a little pitch. It's wonderful, graceful and free.
Soon he's done all the turns and engine checks, and he lets loose with a big, bold victory roll.

CANADA: Niagara Falls, October, 1948

It's been a busy two years for C-GROWL, teaching people to fly. Some students are pretty clumsy, banging the rudder around and landing so hard that the wheels splay out sideways.

After a long day's work, Pat can't resist a little free time sight-seeing over Niagara Falls. Then he climbs up high for a loop.
> Speed to 140 miles per hour;
> Pull back hard on the stick;
> A little rudder to keep the nose straight.

Up and up and up until, hanging upside down at the top of the loop, he eases up on the stick and – the engine stops! Only the sound of the wind.

Not to worry. It happens every time – the engine can't draw gas upside down.
Pass the top of the loop and the nose is pointed at the ground. Rows of peach trees rush up at them.
Then the engine restarts for a graceful pull-out to level again.
Loops are wonderful fun – playing through huge round spaces.

The leaves are turning red and gold. Soon runways and wings will be coated with ice and snow.
There will be hot drinks needed to start the day: coffee for the pilots, heated oil for the planes. Brr.

But this year, C-Growl and Pat won't have to fly in the cold Canadian winter.
They are going to England to show the English how to make Chipmunks.

HORIZONTAL AXIS
Use the elevator for pitch.

Elevator up pushes tail down.

Tail goes down so the nose goes up.

LONGITUDINAL AXIS
Use the ailerons to roll.

Roll around the line from nose to tail.

VERTICAL AXIS
Use the rudder for yaw. Yaw around a line up through the centre.

Tail

Rudder

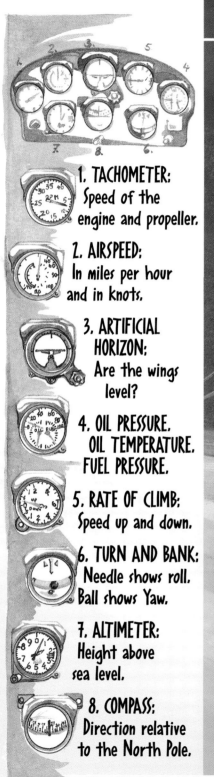

1. TACHOMETER:
Speed of the engine and propeller.

2. AIRSPEED:
In miles per hour and in knots.

3. ARTIFICIAL HORIZON:
Are the wings level?

4. OIL PRESSURE. OIL TEMPERATURE. FUEL PRESSURE.

5. RATE OF CLIMB:
Speed up and down.

6. TURN AND BANK:
Needle shows roll. Ball shows Yaw.

7. ALTIMETER:
Height above sea level.

8. COMPASS:
Direction relative to the North Pole.

ENGLAND: London, June 1949

What a dreadful way for a Chipmunk to travel. Wings off, packed up in crates, crammed into the dark, pitching, sloshing hold of a ship. Planes are meant to be above the ocean – not on it!

Soon after C-Growl arrives, de Havilland in England starts building many Chipmunks. They begin flying for the Royal Air Force, towing gliders for the Swiss Air Force and teaching pilots around the world to fly.

England sure looks different from Canada.
Wiggly roads, thick hedges and small fields; crumpled and cosy.
And rain!
Rain and grumbly, dull clouds – English weather.
It makes the cities greyer and the country greener.

Pat learns the art of scud running;
     twisting around black rain showers;
     flying in the valleys below hill-touching clouds;
     and landing on slick wet runways.
He finds his way by castles, churches and odd-shaped villages as often as following a direct path by compass and time.

Now this is more like it.
A clear sky with the sun setting through the warm haze.
This evening the Prince is learning to fly in C-Growl. As they pass Tower Bridge on the River Thames, just ahead, through the canopy is the Tower of London where English kings and queens used to live. The Prince smiles as he looks down on London.
It's neat to see the places that he knows from the air.

FRANCE: 1950

Pat and C-GROWL are going on a holiday; no students, no gliders, no airforce schedules.

The airforce in Portugal wants Chipmunks to train their pilots. C-GROWL leads a group of six planes to a new Chipmunk factory near Lisbon. They'll just hop the English Channel, sightsee over France, jump the Pyrenees Mountains, wing across Spain and end up in Portugal.

It's a drizzly, grey morning crossing the sea to France but soon the sun and cloud shadows chase across the countryside. The sea sparkles and fishing boats are as colourful as toys. Trains puff steam. We float down to look at castles and cathedrals, heavy walls and deep blue moats, lacy towers and coloured roofs.

The pilots start daydreaming as the formation drones along. Pat pretends C-GROWL is a dragon and the engine noise is roaring fire.

Lazily Pat half wakes up and finds that the cloud has spread until it hides the ground!
Now he's wide awake and worried. While daydreaming, he has wandered off course and lost the other planes.
Is there enough fuel? Is it going to get dark soon? Is there somewhere smooth enough to land?

Look, a gap in the clouds! And, best of all, there's a windsock. So there must be an airfield nearby.
Yes, there it is, two strips cut into the grass in a field.

Pat happily checks the windsock then does a quick circuit.
>	Fly down the airfield, getting lower and lower.
>	Turn past the end and glide gently down, into the wind.
>	Very close to the ground, level out and cut the engine.

Then a bump and a wiggle and he's sliding through the grass in a soft, safe summer evening smelling sweetly of hay. Will they speak English? Is there a sheltered tie-down for C-GROWL? Do they have fuel? Supper and directions for Pat?

In the morning Pat says au revoir. You see? He speaks French already.

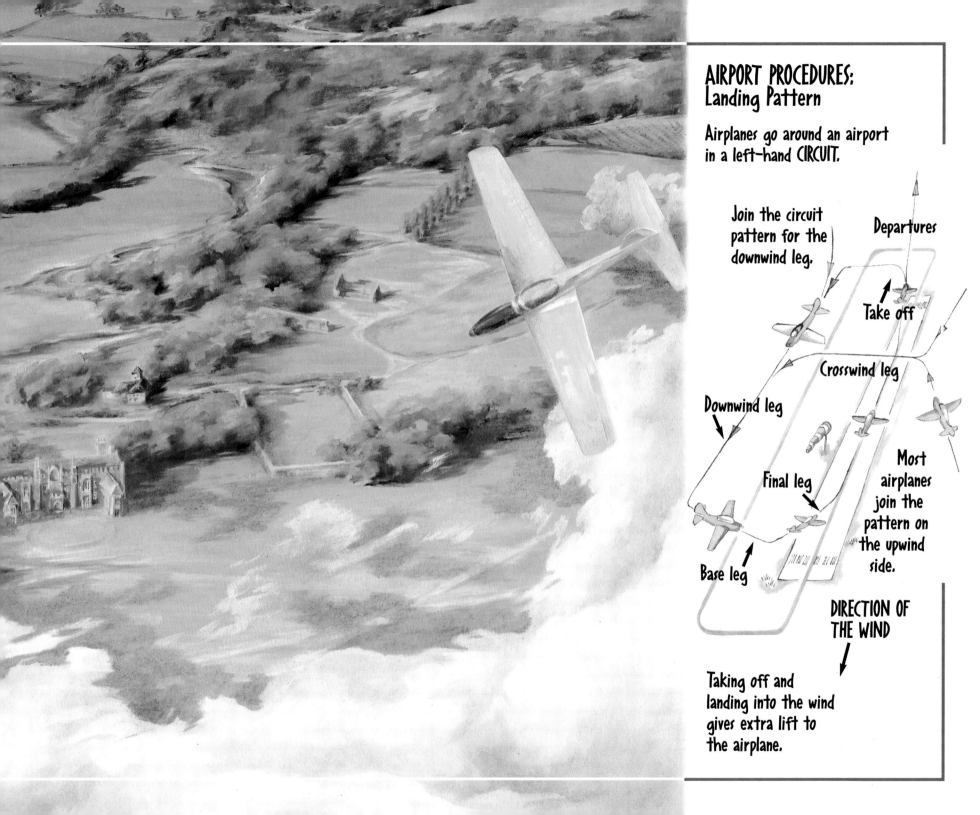

AIRPORT PROCEDURES:
Landing Pattern

Airplanes go around an airport in a left-hand CIRCUIT.

Join the circuit pattern for the downwind leg.

Departures

Take off

Crosswind leg

Downwind leg

Final leg

Base leg

Most airplanes join the pattern on the upwind side.

DIRECTION OF THE WIND

Taking off and landing into the wind gives extra lift to the airplane.

Today C-GROWL's preflight checks are extra important. Especially the compass.

The route from France to Portugal goes between the Cordillera Mountains and the Pyrenees Mountains so navigation has to be exact. To stay on course Pat will need to do some figuring. No bumping into a mountain.

> Smells rise like bubbles through the still morning air.
> Grapes and apricots on the hillsides;
> Salt fish on the coast;
> Barnyards in the valleys.
> The wind off the mountains smells of snow.
> Everything is mixed with the smell of hot engine oil.

Pat starts out over the Bay of Biscay and then flies southwest across Spain. He could just keep going southwest until reaching the coast of Portugal at the Atlantic Ocean. Coasts are easy to find. Then he would turn south and follow the coast around until there is a big river with a big city. That would be Lisbon and up the river from Lisbon is the Chipmunk factory.

That is the safe but clumsy way to navigate. But the Portuguese have been known as wonderful navigators since the days of sailing ships. In Portugal it would be embarrassing to arrive the long way around. So Pat keeps checking the compass. The trouble is that the compass is on the floor of the cockpit. By the time he has leaned forward to look down and let his eyes adjust to the dark, the plane is slowly going off course and rolling. It makes him dizzy in the hot sun.

Excellent. They have arrived right over the Chipmunk factory.

Pat lets down to land with the evening sun behind him. C-GROWL's shadow is straight over the nose.
Nearer to the ground, it gets closer and closer until it is rushing right at the plane.
Without thinking, he bounces into the air to avoid hitting it.

Pretty silly! Perfect navigation around mountains and across countries then scared of his own shadow.

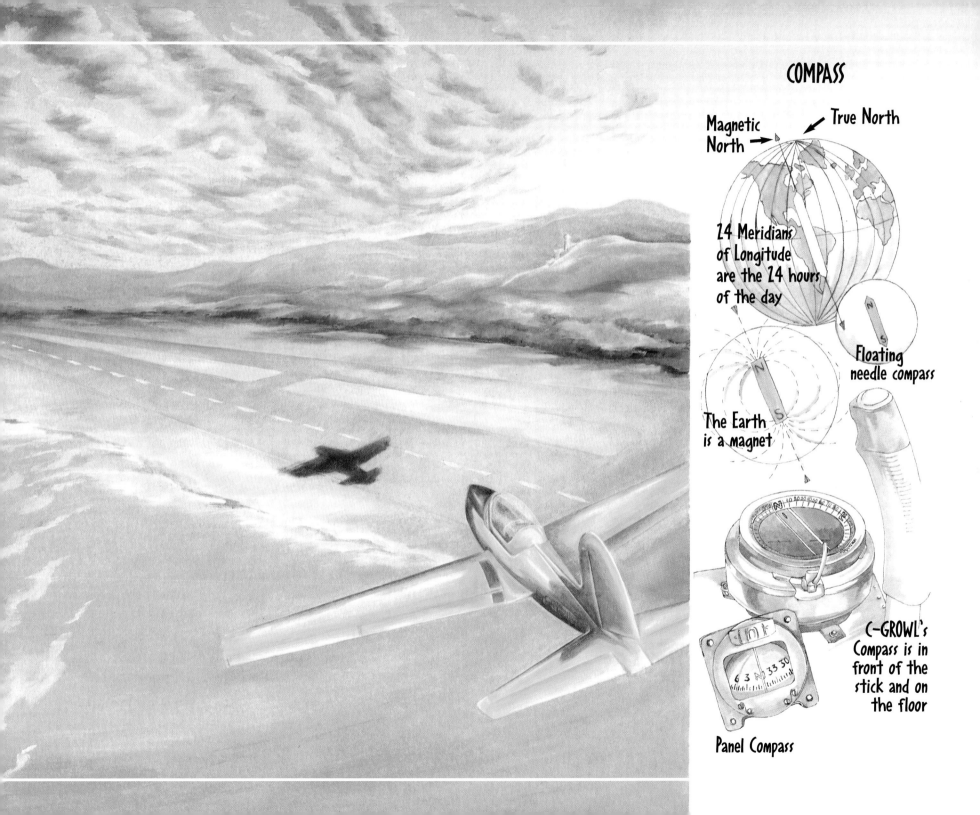

COMPASS

Magnetic North

True North

24 Meridians of Longitude are the 24 hours of the day

Floating needle compass

The Earth is a magnet

C–GROWL's Compass is in front of the stick and on the floor

Panel Compass

CLOUD TYPES

STRATUS clouds are in layers.
Horizontal development.
Dull day clouds.

CUMULUS clouds are
formed by heated
air rising.

Vertical development ↗

NIMBUS: If a cloud is
raining, snowing or
hailing, "nimbus"
is added to the
name.

CUMULONIMBUS

LENS. Wind flows over hills and
mountains in waves that show as
smooth clouds.

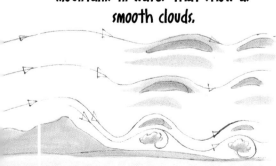

"Aw, come on, watch it! Will somebody please keep those ugly, flat-footed, hump-backed creatures away from that airplane!" Parts of C-GROWL are metal and parts are wood. But the ailerons and tail feathers are only painted cloth. "They're even drooling on the canopy!"

Pat is feeling worn out. It's so hot that it's hard to breathe and the sun is fading C-GROWL's paint.

Wouldn't you know it. The barest place they've ever been to and sand gets in the carburetor. So now they've been waiting a week for a new one to be sent out from England by boat before they can continue their trip down through Africa. It would be faster if they could send it by Chipmunk!

When the carburetor finally arrives, it comes the last bit by camel. Those knobbly-kneed creatures are okay after all. And the camel driver has a gift for Pat – an embroidered saddle cloth for C-GROWL's seat. The leather gets kind of sticky in the heat.

Tomorrow they'll set off south again, fixed and full of fuel.

Just as C-GROWL has been settled down for the quiet desert night with the engine cover tucked on, there is a soft rumble. Slowly it gets louder until a flight of many Chipmunks comes in to land. There will be lots of company for the trip to East Africa.

Everyone rushes and chatters getting fuelled up.

The next day they all take off at dawn while it is still cool, flying in a long loose V. Just like a gaggle of Canada Geese.

SPINS

An airplane stalls when the wings are at too steep an angle to the airflow.

The rudder makes the airplane spin with one wing less stalled than the other.

The spin is stopped by pushing the opposite rudder, and pushing forward to unstall the wings.

The Aerobatic drawing for a spin. (Aresti symbol)

The Chipmunks have flown for days and days, working their way south down the length of Africa.

The pilots talk on their radios, sharing the sights. Over the deserts they're quieter. The empty spaces seem to blow with silence. Those who have been here before tell stories about huge gorillas and snakes. They must all be sleeping in the shade of the trees, out of the hot sun, because we don't see any.

Engines beat a rhythm that mutters and thrums.
    sand dotted with pyramids
         rivers edged with fields
    empty dry deserts
         steamy wet jungles
    spiky cold mountains
         sun-hot plains
    wavy-necked giraffes
         splashing fat hippos
    fan-eared elephants
         crazy-kneed gnus
    flowing soft antelopes
         whirling pink flamingos
It's a long way down to Rhodesia.

Once there, some Chipmunks stay to train new pilots with the Rhodesian Air Schools. Several fly even further to South Africa. Pat's favourite flights are big game spotting. Getting in close to the animals is almost like doing aerobatics again. The elephants wave their ears with irritation as C-GROWL buzzes over them.

Years slip by easily.
One day Pat hears of a real challenge for a Chipmunk, an air race around England!
Soon they are growling along, hurrying back north.

ENGLAND: 1956

Any minute now, they're going to start the King's Cup Air Race around England.

Busy mechanics, anxious pilots, admiring crowds, all smiling and talking in the morning sun.
The airfield is a shimmer of people and all sorts of planes.
> Spindly-legged Austers, as grey and practical as army tents;
> Yellow Piper Super-Cubs with engines sticking out through the sides of their cowls;
> Even some fighter planes who don't really fit this kind of race but have a good time roaring around
> showing off their super-fast dives and streamlined power.

Pat goes to high power with brakes on, quivering, waiting for the start signal.
A flag drops; judges click their watches.
In a yellow flash, C-GROWL is gone.

Pat has practiced racing and navigation and reading the weather signs in the clouds. Concentrating hard, he keeps careful track of the time as they pass the checkpoints and listens on the radio for how the other planes are doing.

The finish line ribbon vibrates in the wind.
High above and three miles out C-GROWL is riding the same tail-wind. Pat drops the nose straight for the finish and picks up even more speed. He screams across the ribbon only fifty feet off the ground then up in a high wing-over loop that brings him gracefully back in line ready to land.
We're the fastest. We're the best.
Smug and happy, Pat and C-GROWL bounce stiff-legged down the runway and turn to be congratulated.

The King's Cup is big and silver, heavy and grand. It is strapped into the front seat like an honoured passenger.

Race Day has been exciting and full; good times, good friends, good airplanes. As the day slowly winds down, the pilots talk and look at airplanes. Tired and contented, Pat is also a little sad because soon C-GROWL will have a new pilot.

That finish-line victory roll was his way of saying goodbye.

He watches the bright machines waddle and squeak across the English daisies, growl and bounce their way into the still evening. Then they lift off gently and set course for their home hangar.

CLOUD LEVELS

High: CIRRO: such as
   cirro-cumulus or
   cirro-stratus or
    CIRRUS

Middle: ALTO: such as
   alto-stratus or
   alto-cumulus or
ALTO CUMULUS
CASTELANUS

Low: STRATUS: such as
   strato-cumulus or
 NIMBO-STRATUS

INDIA: 1958

What a lot of fussing and planning.
Everyone has helped to get C-GROWL ready to fly halfway round the world to a new home in Australia.

Susan, C-GROWL's new ferry pilot, has been making lists for months.
Here's a sample of the C's:

> Chamois: a thin leather that is used to filter any bits out of the gas.
> Cartons of oil: thin for cold weather, thick for hot places.
> Carburetors and spare spark plugs: they don't want to be rescued by camels again or elephants even.
> Compass: re-aligned so it's accurate.
> Charts: it's a fat chart case this trip; Europe, Asia, Oceania and Australia.

The lists go on and on.

C-GROWL has been so checked over and polished that the paintwork glows – smooth and golden.

By now, dozens of airforces use Chipmunks. Often when Susan and C-GROWL land in a new country, they find Canadian-made cousins hard at work.
Airforces love formation flying; several planes flying in patterns beside each other. In India the pilots take off in formation too, thundering upward in a tight arrow. Right beside the leader's tail, Susan watches his wingtip closely. They wheel and climb like a single huge bird.

After a while the formation loosens up and there's time to enjoy the view. There are fantastic forts and palaces but not grey like France. Pink and white, red and blue. A dragon here would want to be crimson and gold.

Back on the ground it's stuffy and hot with noisy shouting and a dusty wind.
C-GROWL is pushed back into a cool dark hangar, echoing with wind and daydreams.

> The oil and filters are changed.
> Dust is washed off, wings are polished.
> The fuel tanks are filled.
> There is still so far to go.

RADIO: an aircraft's "call sign" is spoken in words, not letters.

A – Alfa
B – Bravo
C – Charlie
D – Delta
E – Echo
F – Foxtrot
G – Golf
H – Hotel
I – India
J – Juliett
K – Kilo
L – Lima
M – Mike
N – November
O – Oscar
P – Poppa
Q – Quebec
R – Romeo
S – Sierra
T – Tango
U – Uniform
V – Victor
W – Whiskey
X – X-ray
Y – Yankee
Z – Zulu

RUNWAY MARKINGS

Wind Direction

Runways are named for their compass heading.
31 is for 310°
13 is for 130°

Runway edge: White lights.

Taxiway edge: Blue lights.

Yellow lines: Stop before going on the runway.

Airport Beacon

The RAMP is for getting gas and parking airplanes.

THAILAND: 1958

C-GROWL and Susan hush down low into a gentle golden country.
Orange and yellow spices blow heavy smells through the engine air intakes.
An evening sun glows on ripe rice fields until the hills look like gold brocade cloth threaded with squiggles of turquoise water.
It shines on gold-leaf temples and the wings of gold-covered statues, hung with strings of yellow and orange marigolds.
Orange-robed monks walk through the streets.

Thick patterns of gold on the palace barges conjure up a royal procession. Drums and gongs, flowing yellow-gold silk.
Gold-leaf for C-GROWL? A little vain. Instead Susan gets a new shirt, yellow-gold silk. Just to keep cool, of course.

    Thai dancers sway and twist elegantly.
    Children tug their kites over boat-shaped roofs.
    Hovering, diving colours everywhere.
During the hot afternoons, the air is so full of bounces and shifts that Susan's feet are also dancing – on the rudder pedals.

After a few days they lift off from Thailand in the cool of a pale yellow-green dawn. Chipmunk cousins fly in loose formation until they reach the coast. Then they tilt over to swing back to their day's work and flick their wings goodbye.
C-GROWL flies out over the ocean alone.

It's peaceful, slowly growling past islands, jungly green with long sandy beaches for emergency landings. After Bali, there is only the huge navy-blue ocean, so empty that the earth curves down at the edges on the horizon.

The engine coughs, skips a beat. A second cough.
Then it goes back to its reassuring smooth rumble.
Susan strains to see a change in the line where the sky edges the sea, for some sign of land.

Hazy land on the horizon gets closer at last and they cross the coast of Australia. Landing first on a dirt airstrip, C-GROWL takes on fuel and oil and heads on southeast.

After a while they're flying in the dark, navigating by compass and the stars. But Susan can't see the stars that she's used to. Orion is standing on his head and the North Star has disappeared. A little searching picks out the stars called the Southern Cross. Mostly she follows her compass and feels relieved when the glow of a town and airport lights show up to guide her in.

AUSTRALIA: 1958

Today Susan wakes up slowly after her late night flight. She gets ready lazily, fuels up and finally takes off for Sydney.
The engine hums sleepily in the heat over long, long, long stretches of dry country.
Little whirlwinds of orange dust puff over the empty riverbeds.
Ghost-gum trees seem to float above the ground like balloons anchored by their trunks.

A flock of green and gold cockatoos startles Susan and for a moment she's disoriented.
A quick compass check and – wrong way!
The sun should be on the right for going east; the compass must be wrong! Then she remembers.
This is south of the equator, on the other side of the world and so everything is turned around and the sun is to the north.

The compass was right all along. Of course.
It's just that so much is upside down or backwards here that it's easy to get mixed up.
Still, some things are familiar. People do speak English. Sort of.

Oh no! They've just flown over a herd of camels and now Susan feels she's even got her countries mixed up.

AUSTRALIA: 1959

This is just like home; training dumb beginner pilots for the airforce.
Circuits and landings, bumps and grinds.
Day after day. Month after month.

They have a holiday when visitors come over from New Zealand.
Everyone calls them Kiwis but they're flying Chipmunks so they must be pilots.
The Kiwis talk of boiling mud valleys, dawn-pink glaciers and herding deer down steep mountainsides.

C-GROWL and Susan listen to their stories and get restless to be travelling again.
Time for a new job.

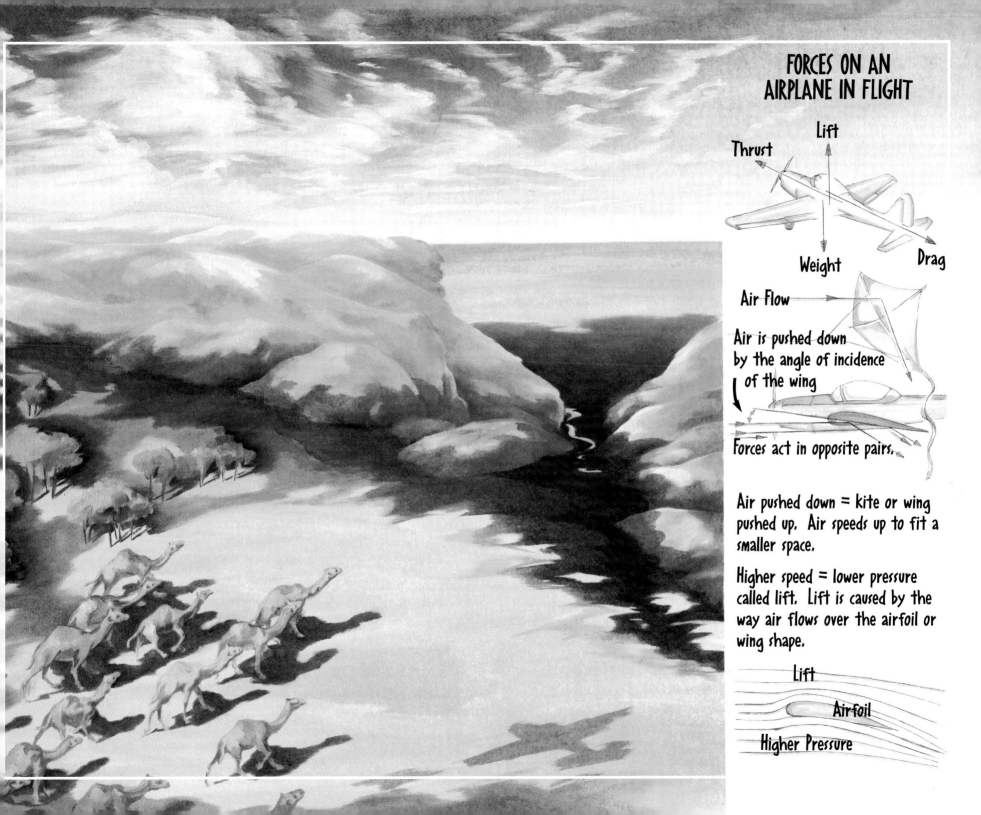

FORCES ON AN AIRPLANE IN FLIGHT

Lift

Thrust

Weight

Drag

Air Flow

Air is pushed down
by the angle of incidence
of the wing

Forces act in opposite pairs.

Air pushed down = kite or wing
pushed up. Air speeds up to fit a
smaller space.

Higher speed = lower pressure
called lift. Lift is caused by the
way air flows over the airfoil or
wing shape.

Lift

Airfoil

Higher Pressure

Throttle in the cockpit regulates air flow.

Pump

Throttle lever in the engine sends the message to the carburetor and also activates the fuel pump.

The carburetor uses the airflow to mix air and gas into a vapour. This explodes in the pistons and drives the engine.

AUSTRALIAN OUTBACK: 1962

C-GROWL has become a civilian, sold to a tiny town in the Australian outback.
One storey houses with round-shouldered tin roofs. Roads leading vaguely off to out-of-sight sheep stations.

Every day Susan flies over long distances of hot, flat spaces wrinkled by low lines of hills.
Crazy piles of enormous boulders look like they were heaped up by giants. From 6,000 feet up they look just like the rock piles pulled out of the farmers' fields in Canada.

The pre-flight checklist has grown: – snakes caught in the brakes?
                                        – bottles of water for emergency landings?
And for the Flying Doctor's regular check-up trips the list grows again:
                                        – splints, bandages, medical bag?
Or how about strapping a guitar into the passenger seat? Music is a harmony of engine growls, wind whistling and the music teacher singing as he flies out to a rare lesson with a station kid.

No rain has its nice sides.
Back country nights are spent peacefully under a starry sky. Engine maintenance is done in the shade of a gum tree.

Best of all, Susan likes chasing sheep. They're hard to find scattered over the huge stations.
        Yee-hah!   Git along little dogies.
Sheep bounce and scramble wildly away from the noisy sky-cowboy.
The roar of C-GROWL's engine scares them out from the shade of bushes and behind rocks.
        Now the sheep-herders on horses can run them along into the shearing pens.

Susan circles in to land in the late, slanty sun near the wool barns, laughing at the skittering sheep, shorn bare and silly looking. As the plane touches the dirt, a rock catches the wheel.
Whack! Down goes a wing.
The propeller hits the hard ground with a ringing clank.
And C-GROWL sits in a cloud of dust, engine silent, listening to thousands of sheep baa-ing, laughing back.

C-GROWL is pushed into the back of a quiet, dark shearing barn to wait for a mechanic.
Wool drifts in around the wheels and settles like snow on the cowl.

AUSTRALIA: 1989

The mechanic never arrives.

Years pass and C-GROWL just gets older and dustier. Fabric dries out, paint flakes off.
The barn is deserted and weeds grow around the door.

Sitting in that dry, dark barn, does C-GROWL dream?
Does he still play in clouds, zipping up the dark sides, tobogganing down the sunny sides, flicking knife-edge through cloud chasms, charging straight into the little ones and watching them dissolve in his prop-wash?
City cowboys, country pilots, flying farmers, airforce aerobats.
Hushed hangars, star-quiet fields, empty wool barns.

Airplanes don't dream – but pilots do.
One day, there's a banging and clumping, a sudden rush of sunlight.
A friendly Australian called Glen swings open the barn door.
He walks around all the airplane parts on the floor and strokes the side of the fuselage. After that he's a bit nosier.
He pokes ailerons, rattles wings and shakes the landing gear. He smiles and stomps out.
What was that all about?

Next morning Glen brings many friends and a big flat-bed truck.
They shout and heave and load up every bit of airplane they can find in the barn.

Glen's big square face grins.
He is dreaming of air shows.

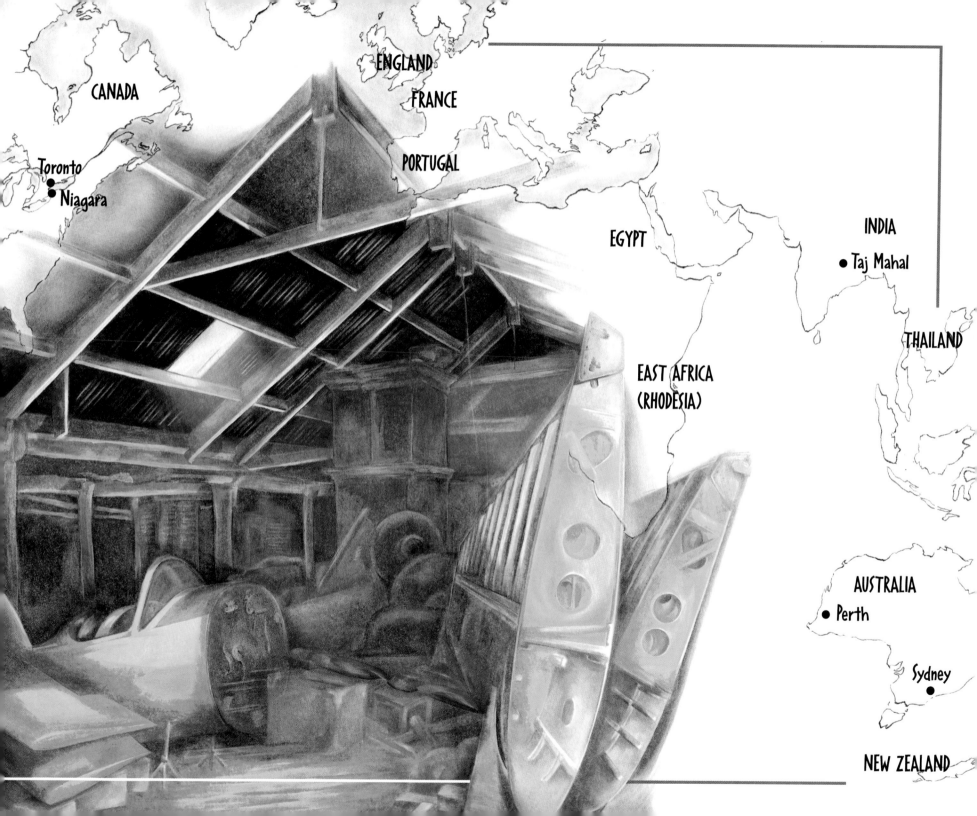

CANADA

Toronto
Niagara

ENGLAND

FRANCE

PORTUGAL

EGYPT

EAST AFRICA
(RHODESIA)

INDIA

Taj Mahal

THAILAND

AUSTRALIA

Perth

Sydney

NEW ZEALAND

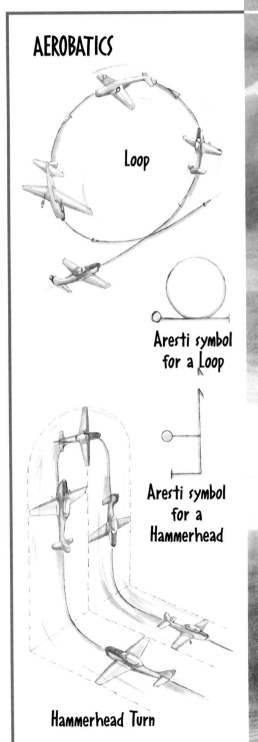

AEROBATICS

Loop

Aresti symbol
for a Loop

Aresti symbol
for a
Hammerhead

Hammerhead Turn

First C-GROWL needs a good re-build.
Everything is pulled apart and labelled. Then the thousands of pieces are each fixed and cleaned and tested.
>New wood for dried and cracked bits.
>Everything rubber is replaced.
>Leather too, except that Glen keeps the wrinkled, friendly leather seats.

Slowly, enough pieces are in perfect shape.
The assemblies are fitted together and then the systems are tested.
It's several long, careful years before C-GROWL is rolled outside. Sunshine and an audience after months of hangar gloom.

>More tests!   Engine tests. C-GROWL roars and purrs for hours.
>Taxi tests.   Waggling up and down the runway.
>Yup. Everything works. When do they get to take off?

Finally they're flying. Up high, wonderful and breezy. C-GROWL is an airplane again.

Hoo-boy, Glen is full of wild ideas. Loops and rolls aren't enough – no way.
C-GROWL's wings spin with new maneuvers and new names. Like the Hammerhead;
>straight up until the plane is just barely stopped;
>pushing on the right rudder to keep from wobbling;
>balanced as delicately as a tight-rope walker, then BANG
Glen stomps on the left rudder and cartwheels around the left wingtip until he's pointing straight down.
It's not only hammer shaped at the top but it flicks C-GROWL's tail like a hammerhead shark.

When a maneuver lines up just right, the Chipmunk runs into its own wake turbulence at the end.
Glen gets a little bounce, a funny nudge to congratulate him and wake him up ready for the next maneuver.

It gets to be fun flying inverted or watching the colours of sea, sky and beach whirl.
The engine sputters with the giggles in the loops.

It seems like they're ready to show off in front of a crowd when C-GROWL gets through a rolling circle,
>like a wiggling puppy chasing its own tail.
Then whappo, a snap roll; twisting the tail hard, like a sideways spin with power, yeouch!

SYDNEY: 1996

Welcome to the Sydney Air Show.

It's fifty years since the first flight of a Chipmunk way back in Canada.
So this year's guest of honour is C-GROWL, flying in the clear, loud sunshine of Australia.

A big holiday crowd is watching – shorts and suntanned legs, big-brimmed hats and sunglasses.
Sails bounce across sparkles on the water.
The Harbour Bridge and the Opera House, old and new, are both as elegant as airplanes.
That great, spidery bridge makes a perfect landmark for lining up air show maneuvers.

Glen switches on his new smoke-tank.
Soon a puffy streamer pours out behind C-GROWL, drawing white pictures on the purple-blue sky.
Huge circles and lines from the loops and cubans,
     Tight corkscrews for a snap roll.

Tricky maneuvers flow smoothly,
     roll and wiggle, swoop and soar, flip and spin.
High on top of a loop the plane holds its breath with the crowd
     then roars back down low over the sailboats.
They're playing, dancing in the air.

A voice on the radio reminds Glen that it's time to finish.
One last show-off, a rolling circle, spirals of smoke twisting round into a donut.
Then a fast, swinging victory roll and a wing-wag goodbye.

Beautiful.

Sharp, black nose pointing at the sky.

Long, tapered wings, bright yellow, flashing in the sun.

*We acknowledge the financial support of the Government of Canada through
the Book Publishing Industry Development Program for our publishing activities.*

Vanwell Publishing Limited
1 Northrup Crescent,
PO Box 2131
St. Catharines, ON
L2R 7S2

Printed in Belgium

02 01 00 99   4 3 2 1

Canadian Cataloguing in Publication Data

McHaffie, Nat
  C-Growl, the daring little airplane

ISBN 1-55125-015-2 (bound)
ISBN 1-55125-019-5 (pbk.)

1. Chipmunk (Training plane) – Juvenile literature.
2. Aeronautics – Flights – Juvenile literature. 3. Voyages
and travels – Juvenile literature.   I. Title.

TL686.D4M26 1998   J629.13   C98-931903-2

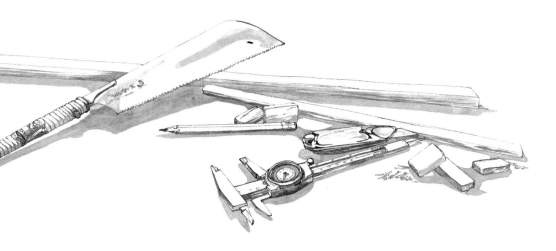

For

R.   J.   F.

for the

Romeo Juliett Foxtrot

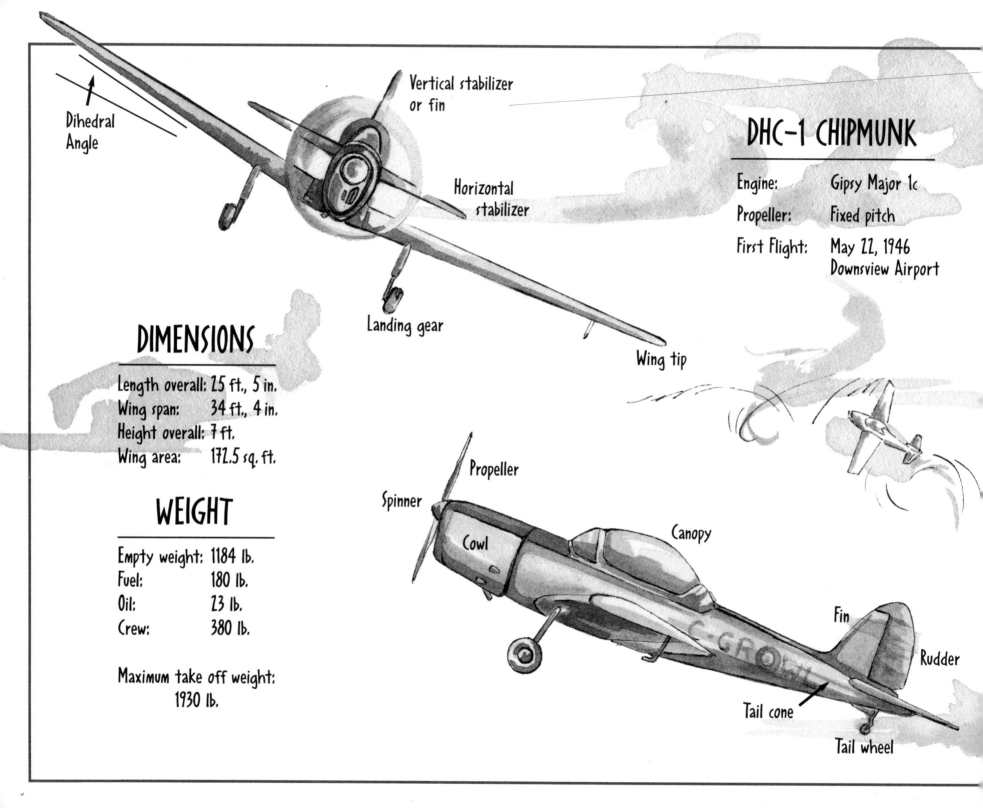

Dihedral Angle

Vertical stabilizer or fin

Horizontal stabilizer

Landing gear

Wing tip

DHC-1 CHIPMUNK

Engine: Gipsy Major 1c
Propeller: Fixed pitch
First Flight: May 22, 1946
             Downsview Airport

DIMENSIONS

Length overall: 25 ft., 5 in.
Wing span: 34 ft., 4 in.
Height overall: 7 ft.
Wing area: 172.5 sq. ft.

WEIGHT

Empty weight: 1184 lb.
Fuel: 180 lb.
Oil: 23 lb.
Crew: 380 lb.

Maximum take off weight:
       1930 lb.

Propeller

Spinner

Cowl

Canopy

Fin

Rudder

Tail cone

Tail wheel